THE IMPOTENT

THE IMPOTENT

M. MUBASHAR NAWAZ

KHURRAM SHAHZAD

First Edition: 2020
Publish by: Sanjh

سانجھ

SANJH
PUBLICATIONS

Title Design: **Saboor Sultan**

Dedication

To all the children suffering around the world.

AUTHORS' NOTE

Drama has a history of being the most influential piece of art as it could arrest the minds, control the hearts, and enchant the audience in such a way that they start identifying themselves with the characters. The presentation of direct speech in a drama squeezes the distance between the audience and the characters. Besides, it could be said that drama is as ancient as human civilization; the greater the history, the greater the responsibility a dramatist feels. We have strived, without being influenced by a particular author or age and without going out of the parameters of drama, to be spontaneous and indigenous but the echo of human concerns discussed by various authors can also be felt in our drama.

Moreover, the state of English drama in Pakistan has always been precarious; either it has not been written or the written not performed. Even the availability of theatres in Pakistan has been scanty and the few stages available have not been appropriately equipped--one of the biggest reasons behind drama's being unnourished. Therefore, the theatre in Pakistan could neither refine nor elevate the minds. Away from theatre, TV dramas, owing to commercialism and the rat-race between different channels, are very much burgeoning and center of the whole attention making the theatre lag behind. Some of the writers and directors have struggled to revive theatrical culture in Pakistan; a few of their attempts have quite been successful, our purpose is also to be the part of the culture which is striving to take theatre a step ahead.

Collaborative writing in Literature hasn't been in much vogue, though it has been experimented sometimes. The few instances we find are those where two or more authors have written one piece of literature as some scenes of Marlowe's Doctor Faustus are said to have been interpolated later. Our experimenting with collaborative writing has produced a product of two minds with sheer compatibility; for both of us look at human condition with almost the same lens. Each sentence of ours is well thought, well discussed, and we have written it together. Neither of us can say "the thought is mine", rather we say "it's ours".

Introspecting the world, we often come across many philosophical as well as social issues. Many a time, we two-together go into the trance of sadness and discuss with each other "the grunt and sweat of a weary life". A photograph of a child in a miserable condition worked as a stimulus and made us discuss the scheming in the world around us where innocent children are the sufferers who have no part in creating the mess around them. The idea developed with the question, "who is responsible?", and we looked forward to work on it and shape it as a play.

M. MUBASHAR NAWAZ

&

KHURRAM SHAHZAD

FOREWORD

Blaise Pascal said:

"The eternal silence of infinite spaces frightens me."

Iqbal says:

This sky, this world of solitude

Scares me the width of the desert

Human imagination couldn't fathom the immense vastness of time and space for human existence is trivial and insignificant in the larger scheme of universe. The shadow of suffering and sorrow always haunts man and everyone is born to bear his share of the griefs. On the hind-side, one can hear Nietzsche's whisper, "to live is to suffer".

Man has been sent to the world against his will to encounter untoward circumstances, inappropriate conditions and uncertain happenings. The journey through this is going on and he wrestles with the troubles of life, puts his courage on trial and, finally, being lost in swirls, gives in and collapses in particles. In fact, the solid wall of trials and tribulations has surrounded mankind, for a whole generation which struggles laboriously to thin the Herculean wall down for the coming generations, but their struggle goes in vain—the wall, though seems to be thinned down, remains the same. Every man, according to his capacity, takes part in this incessant strife but the trickery of time multiples it.

Instead of becoming the part of the herd, some people contemplate that, despite all human evolution, Adam's children are falling a prey to the atrocious life where demons of hunger dance wildly, plagues and incurable diseases sting human feeling, the brutality of the strong feeds upon the bone marrow of the weak, and intoxicatedly ruthless power of the capitalists crushes the nations. Ionesco, having seen all this, had rightly said:

"I have no other images of the world, aside from those which express evanescence and hardness, vanity and anger, nothingness or hideous and useless hate. Existence has continued to appear to me in this way. Vain and sordid furors, cries suddenly stifled by silence, shadows swallowed up forever in night."

By observing all this, man searches for meaningfulness of his continuous yet futile efforts or gives up his struggle. Sometimes he finds solace in religion, escape in history, meaning in culture or submits to societal pressure. He, at times, losing faith in the 'cherished' values, steers onto the path of futility and worthlessness. Such moments in human life make the genius Sartre utter:

"Everything has been figured out except how to live."

Such an individual travels on a new path, designs new principles for his living, challenges established rules and concocted principles of society but society does not approve such behavior and brands this attitude rebellious. The rebel calls thinking patterns, customs and traditions, ways of discussion into question and discarding them struggles to find out novel horizons. Here, he has to bear the reaction of society. The individual desires to keep the 'power to choose' to himself while society cannot deprive itself of the fundamental right to enforce its will. This battle ends with the submission of either of the two. If the individual submits, he becomes the part of the society. If society succumbs to his will, it makes the person its part.

Aalif, the main character of the drama under discussion, perceived the same that the world around him is replete with sorrows and it leaves no space for deliverance. Every person has to bear agonies. The alive will endure the agony of death. Thus, the fountain of trouble is life itself as Buddha perceived that desires put humanity into sorrows and concluded that man should give up wishes to keep sorrows away. Aalif also feels that man embraces sorrow because he's alive. No life, no pain.

Existence is sorrow, the growth of existence is sorrow

Life is sorrow, death is sorrow

To be is sorrow, not to be is sorrow

Stasis is sorrow, perpetuity is sorrow
O my dear! all is sorrow

      (Last Sermon of Buddha by Aslam Ansari)

The protagonist desires to lessen the pains from the world. He devises, as far in his prowess, a scheme that the coming generation must be redeemed from those pains. If they are born, they will experience troubles, if not born, protected from them. He decides not to produce a child. If the world is topsy-turvy, it should cease to be as Bahadur Shah Zafar pronounces:

Zafar! Affliction is the ever-thriving world

As wasteland would have been created such a dwelling

His decision provides him mental gratification, but the proclamation of the very choice appalls the society. The continuity of children is a guarantee to the social salvation. No children will lead society to its own death. His voice trembles the chambers of society. The foundation of family, religion and feudalism stumbles. "Down is the courage of gods." To fend their rule, they unleash their power onto him but he, in the words of Kierkegaard, considers individual's discretion and 'what is true for me" vital and asserts that no ultimate can decide for him. He feels that he has every right to live his life according to his principles. Aalif doesn't want his offspring whereas the society for its salvation is determined to hunt the emerging example down. On this conflict, the drama *"The Impotent"* erupts. How the story of this drama progresses, how it ends, one comes to know after reading it? Meanwhile, for the curious reader, it can be said, in this drama, the dramatic action progresses exquisitely, and the subject has been justified fully. The presentation of Aalif's point of view and society's reaction is fabulous. At one point, the reader seems to agree with Aalif's views, and this is the point where the shifting feelings of Aalif show that an artistic drama is not one dimensional rather it keeps on unfurling its layers.

The subject matter of this drama is innovative, and it has been given full opportunity to expand and to explicate all consequences. To continue with such a philosophical subject matter is challenging but the authors have carried it out tremendously. The spectator will remain in the spell of the play till the end and the reader will be restless till the last lines. It is hoped if this play is staged, it will be a successful one.

Muhammad Abbas

CHARACTERS

AALIF	*The Protagonist*
NABIGHA	*AALIF's Wife*
HAARIS	*AALIF's Friend*
FATHER	*AALIF's Father*
MOTHER	*AALIF's Mother*
AADAM	*A Boy*

&

Others

To have committed every crime but that of being a father.

E. M. Cioran

A man who held a newborn child in his hands approached a holy man. "What shall I do with this child?" he asked; "it is wretched, misshapen, and does not have life enough to die." "Kill it!" shouted the holy man with a terrible voice; "and then hold it in your arms for three days and three nights to create a memory for yourself. Never again will you beget a child this way when it is not time for you to beget. "When the man had heard this, he walked away, disappointed, and many people reproached the holy man because he had counseled cruelty; for he had counseled the man to kill the child. "But is it not crueler to let it live" asked the holy man.

Friedrich Nietzsche

THE IMPOTENT

ACT I SCENE I

The scene is in a very small room that seems to be stuffed with darkness; the paint on the walls is so dark as to choke the presence of light. There are two doors and only one window--that opens to the street; one of the doors opens to TV lounge and the other to the street. Just beside the door to TV Lounge, a few chairs and a sofa are set in an unsymmetrical way. Above the sofa, there is a bookshelf where books are piled in bookshelves; classical in the upper-shelf and modern in the lower. Newspapers, his shoes and clothes are spread everywhere and an ashtray brimful of ash and cigarettes is lying on the floor. There are a few paintings on the walls. One of them is in the hands of Aalif, a frail fellow with long, dark black but disheveled hair, rough beard, and deep gloomy eyes. He, with a shattered visage and pained eyes, is gazing at the painting. The painting is of a little boy in rags, carrying his baggage on head and standing in a far stretched desert with an innocent face but inquiring eyes.

AALIF:

How can you see this,

THE IMPOTENT

      If this is the existence?
I'd prefer ceasing it— —- not with hands But
with will.

My heart grieves when I see

The world's doom before doom

Where hunger eats a few

Where war terrorises

Where killing is a sport

No one humanises

Where childhood cries

Among bombs and death

Where youth strives

For a day's breath

When to see is to grieve

And to know is to suffer

When to live is a hell

And to breathe is tougher

Why should I not— —stop the beast in me, The
desire to reproduce But.... What of the
instinctual Drive of having sex?

      Something should be done!!!

Something should be done!!

To save my generation

I think.....

They should not come to existence.

They should not come to existence. *(He seems out of himself, takes out a cigarette, lights it and starts taking long puffs).*

ACT I SCENE II

The scene shifts to TV lounge where Aalif's family is having tea and gossiping with laughter out-loud. The lounge with its door and a window opening to courtyard is wide and neatly furnished with sofas properly arranged in a semi-circular way leaving a plenty of room in and around. A huge LED is set on the walls in front of sofas and news about a missile attack killing hundreds of children seems to be overwhelmed by the apathetic laughter. The door opens and Aalif comes out of his room mumbling.

AALIF: *(baffled)* I would not have a child.

I would not have a child

(All are engrossed in gossips while Aalif's voice is suppressed. He goes to his wife, grabs her hand, takes her a bit away and whispers)

AALIF: I want to talk to you, spare a moment for me.

NABIGHA: I am rather busy. You always have something to tell.

AALIF: But this something is severe enough to kill me from inside. The pain is high; it can make me die.

NABIGHA: *(jokingly)* But you aren't dead yet.

AALIF: Yeah! Apparently.
NABIGHA: *(casually)* What apparently! You are here in front of me, complete, alive, talking, arguing. AALIF: How do you know I'm alive, complete? Look   deep.

NABIGHA: *(lightly)* Don't philosophize things. I'm not interested in your mumbo-jumbo ideas. Do what you have come for.

AALIF: *(pleadingly)* Everybody can't but you can make me out. You seem the only one I can share with. I can't help. Otherwise things will get out of reach. The lion will start roaring and it'll devour all. Being human, I may suffer for myself but not for others.

NABIGHA: *(impatiently)* Would you please come back from your stupor and tell me what the matter is?

AALIF: I've decided something.

NABIGHA: It must be something mind-boggling. *(She tries to release her arm, but he grips it even harder)*

AALIF: No, No! It's not like that.

(After a pause)

NABIGHA: *(restlessly)* What is it then?

AALIF: I have, after much contemplation and observation, made up my mind not to have children.

NABIGHA: *(shouting)* Have you got out of your mind! What rubbish are you talking about! You seem possessed!

AALIF: *(lowering the pitch of his voice)* Life in itself is a monstrous witch and I can't sacrifice my children to it. It is a she-snake that needs its own snakelets for survival. If it is meant to eat, why on earth does it, after all, give birth to them. I can't let it devour what is part of me, what is my flesh and blood.

NABIGHA: O come on, Aalif! Children are the symbol of life.

AALIF: O really! I don't think so. Life has its existence on the planet since the time immemorial. We are very recent. Man's existence is essential for life looks quite absurd.

NABIGHA: *(indignantly)* You will definitely get oblivious of these irrational conjectures when I'll make you face your father and your mother. I thought you were coward in front of them but you are timid in life too. How pathetic of you! AALIF: You misconstrue my reverence to cowardice, but   this time, I am resolute in my decision.

NABIGHA: I know your resolution. You can't impose your decision upon me. It involves me and I am desirous of a child.

AALIF: *(vaguely)* It's better for our child.

NABIGHA: *(shocked)* How can it be better for the one
        unborn? Be a man!

AALIF: Try to …. (she cuts him off)

NABIGHA: *(annoyingly)* Please! You know what
        happens to a lady who bears no child in our
        society.

AALIF: I can, but…

(She gets her arm released, goes to Aalif's parents who are laughing with each other and casually watching TV. Aalif stands for a while, mumbles and leaves. Nabigha shrieks at the top of her voice)

NABIGHA: Look, what your son is saying!
(They startlingly turn their heads to her)
MOTHER: What happened?

NABIGHA: *(irritably)* He does not want to have a child.

FATHER: What are you saying, daughter! It cannot be true. No one can be so much irresponsible and foolish.

NABIGHA: No, father. He has said so and says he's resolute this time.

FATHER: *(angrily)* I know his resolutions; he's bloody good-for-nothing and wants to rid of his filial responsibilities. He does nothing, earns nothing, and knows he won't be able to bring up his children. I can't let him do it.

MOTHER: You people should listen to me. At least, my son isn't like this. He will change his mind, I know him.

NABIGHA: Mother! This is your illusion. He's become a mysteriously odd man. Recently, I, sometimes, get terrified living with him. He is mostly not what he seems to be. He keeps on talking alone, remains silent for hours, and doesn't like to meet or face people. I'm unable to make out what he is made of.

FATHER: Some people have enigmatic personalities, but his enigma is crossing limits.

[silence]

FATHER: My life has been a series of struggles but I have borne all for the sake of him. He is the only heir to me and now, look, what he's doing?

MOTHER: Nabigha, go and call him. Let us convince him if he has started thinking idiosyncratically. *(She goes out to call Aalif. After some moments, he enters numbly and sits)*

FATHER: Son, what I have heard of is true?

(He remains silent) FATHER: Hello, mister! I'm talking to you.

AALIF: Well...... Yes.

FATHER: Would you change your mind, or will we have to change it for you?

AALIF: Have I no power even on my mind?

FATHER: You have when it is sane and reasonable.

AALIF: How do I or you know what is sane or reasonable?

FATHER: I'm your father and I know.

AALIF: *(ethereally)* Your knowing has ruined me and my life.

FATHER: What the hell are you talking about?

AALIF: Truth.

FATHER: *(surprised)* What truth? Do you mean to say that I have been living through all this to ruin your life? I've spent my sleepless nights for your wellbeing. I've committed even some crimes and sins for your sake. Is this the reward you are paying me?

AALIF: What if you have not given birth to me! What if I had been a pebble, or a stone, or a tree or a dog! What if I had been a cloud or a drop of rain! What if I had not been born! I would have loved to be anything but a human being. To live is to suffer. You are responsible for my being here.

FATHER: *(sighs) (to Aalif's mother)* Have you listened to what he is blurting out? This son of ours has gone mad. He is going against the law of nature. He is revolting and heading to the way of ultimate damnation.

MOTHER: My son! For us, you are the only hope. I beseech you not to do this.

FATHER: You are living in fool's paradise. You alone cannot change the scheme of things.

AALIF: *(sarcastically)* At least, it is a paradise not hell.

[pause]

I'm not revolting against anyone, how can I? An inconsequential sperm! I'm trying to do what I can to save someone from suffering.

NABIGHA: What did you marry me for, to satisfy the desires of the animal inside you? It is the animal that is the cause of all sufferings not nature.

AALIF: No birth, no animal, no suffering.

[pause]

Even the mother earth is burdened and is keen to shed us off. It wants to breathe; we are choking it, strangling it. Before it explodes, we must do something to unburden it. I'm looking at the larger picture.

MOTHER: Keep your larger picture with you, we want an heir.

FATHER: People will call you impotent. Have you ever thought of the consequences of your action?

AALIF: Consequences often remain unknown and I'm ready to bear all of them. Hell with people! They enjoy when we suffer. I won't give them a chance to savour.

NABIGHA: I won't let you enjoy either.

AALIF: And I will revel in breaking the cycle--- the cycle
of suffering.

FATHER: You won't, you flea!

AALIF: *(adamantly)* I will. At least, I'll try to. I won't
become the part of the herd like you.

(He goes out)

FATHER: *(helplessly)* Look at him!

NABIGHA: *(repentantly)* Love for this man blinded me.
Now, things are getting out of control. Father!

Find a way or we will lose him.

MOTHER: He wasn't like that. This is unbelievable.

Should we take him to a psychiatric?

FATHER: I don't know.

NABIGHA: My family, my brothers are leading a healthy,
happy life. Why can't he? Why can't we because
of him?

[aside] Once he used to say the world looks
beautiful when he looks into my eyes. My
presence was enough for him. That charm was
ephemeral. Now he's aloof, always seems
somewhere else.

MOTHER: But he doesn't have what your brothers have
wealth, property, social status, friends, luxurious life.

Anyone can be happy with these things. Happiness can be bought nowadays. Your family can buy it, my son can't.

NABIGHA: You are loading things, this isn't the case, I think he's above these things now.

FATHER: None is above materiality. Millions are born in misery and die in it but people with affluence keep on multiplying their trash. NABIGHA: He could do that but he didn't. His failures shouldn't play havocs with our lives.

MOTHER: You should sooth him instead of........ FATHER: *(interrupting)* Would you please stop arguing and blaming each other?

MOTHER: Why don't you understand? I can't see my only son wasting his life like that.
FATHER: Can we undo what is destined to happen? Let's call his friend.

MOTHER. He may help us get out of this mire.

 (Father calls Haaris. Bell rings but he does not pick the phone.)

FATHER: He is an ass! *(Calls again. Haaris picks up the phone)*

FATHER: Why don't you pick up the phone, we have a terrible situation here.

HAARIS' VOICE: What happened, Uncle. Is everything all right?

FATHER: Your friend!

HAARIS' VOICE: *(worriedly)* What happened to him?

FATHER: Come to our home, I will try to explain. I think you are the only friend of his we can share with. HAARIS' VOICE: Sure, Uncle, I'm coming in half an   hour.

FATHER: He's coming but I still believe people are what they are. Nothing can change them from inside.

NABIGHA: Society can.

FATHER: Cowards only.

NABIGHA: All are cowards then?

FATHER: May be.

NABIGHA: Are you with him or with us?

FATHER: I don't know.

[silence]

(They wait till the doorbell rings and the mother opens the door. Haaris enters. He is a short but healthy fellow. His face is round with stubble beard and intelligent yet a bit mischievous looks) HAARIS: *(inquiringly)* Where is he?

FATHER & MOTHER: *(together)* He is in his room.

FATHER: Listen son, I think it's not easy to explain but let me try. He is expressing his pointless idea that he won't produce a child forever.

HAARIS: *(shocked)* What! That's ridiculous!

MOTHER: You are our only hope. Do something.

 Change his mind. He is getting incomprehensible.

HAARIS: He usually listens to me but this worries me. I really am shocked with what could he have on his mind this time.

MOTHER: We have tried but he is not convinced. He has his conviction and logic we can't encounter with arguments. Please help us in this. I'll bless you.

HAARIS: Ok, I'm going to him. I'll talk to him.

(He goes to Aalif's room)

ACT I SCENE III

The scene is in Aalif's room. He inhales the smoke of cigarette, relishes it and exhales.

AALIF:

What I think is unthinkable

What I believe is unbelievable

Why can't they see the seeable

Why can't they feel the feel-able

The earth is the soma of pain

Where the wise do strive and go insane

Where words are fake and a waste are deeds

Where flowers are few and more are weeds

Where beast do pounce on kids and rape

Where harshness itself does reshape

Where lust's religion, sex is creed Where
none can satisfy his greed.

How can one be happy?

We either have to be bold enough

To wade into the sea of uncertainty

And be an uncertain part of chaos Or....
We.....

Suffer— suffer, methinks, from existence

When the beginning is to be born

And ultimate end is to die,

When the middle is either to suffer

Or to struggle fighting with suffering

How can one be satisfied

With the idea of life-hereafter

—- the assumable?

Even if we are How can we

survive for heaven (the reward

of virtue)?

(A knock at the door is heard and Haaris enters)

HAARIS: *(looking around)* How messy! How chaotic!

AALIF: Yes! It is messy. It is chaotic.

[silence]

HAARIS: *(jests)* You really know how to get attention!
You freak!

[silence]

HAARIS: *(ironically)* I heard you are on a great grand
mission.

[silence]

HAARIS: *(seriously)* Ok, tell me what's in your head.

AALIF: A storm.

HAARIS: *(with a grin)* What storm?
AALIF: A volcano, a tornado, may be .... what else?

HAARIS: I'm not getting what's going on with you?

AALIF: Even I'm not getting.

HAARIS: Who will?

AALIF: I don't know.

(Aalif's face seems withered away with eyes barren and stagnant as if finding something that never is and never will be. His turning to Haaris shocks him).

HAARIS: O my God!

[pause]

AALIF: *(inquiringly)* Why? My God?

HAARIS: What's the point?

AALIF: I'm searching a point but the quest is pointlessly pointless.

HAARIS: Searching is believing that there is a point.
AALIF: Searching is, in fact, making belief that there is a point but actually it's like bumping one's head into a wall.

HAARIS: What exactly are you at?

AALIF: I'm trying to do "the nothing".

HAARIS: That's fuss!

AALIF: *(admittedly)* Yes, that's fuss!

[pause]

AALIF: What difference does it make to the world if I don't do anything.

HAARIS: Then, why are you here?

AALIF: I'm here because of others. I'm here because I have been brought against my will. I'm here because I did not know about this miserable world. I'm here because I am powerless. I'm here because I am unable to undo what has been done to me. I'm here because you people do not set me free. I'm here and I should not be. What difference it would've been to the limitless and unfathomable universe if I had not been here. Why am I a necessity for the world? What difference does a particle of sand make to the whole desert? What difference does it make when one is born and the other dies? What difference does your happiness make to others? What difference does my depressed being make to others? Do great actions of the great make you happy or bring any change to the world? The world without technology needed something and the world loaded with technology also needs something. People suffered in the science less world and they are equally suffering in the scientifically

advanced world. In the evolution of humans an civilizations, human sufferings also evolved and transformed but remained consistent. Happy is the one who's never born. Happy is the one who's never born.

(Haaris remains silent for quite a time) HAARIS: *(giggles mockingly)* You are reversing the entire purpose of existence. Don't you think it's illogical?

AALIF: I think existence itself is very illogical; for one is born but to die and, in between, keeps on questioning his existence — the existence in which the meaning is either unfound or the found is futile.

HAARIS: You mean we all should cease to be?

AALIF: Yes, Die!

HAARIS: What do you think about death....... a solution, an escape or a solace?

AALIF: An end!

HAARIS: An end? To what?

AALIF: An end to the quest of happiness that is never found. An end to solace that is never achieved.

(After a long pause)

HAARIS: Hmm! So death is an end?

AALIF: Yes, it......... is ...... an end. We should develop a habit ofstrangulating phoenix.

HAARIS: Strangulating phoenix means strangulating life?

AALIF: When life is punishment, it must be strangulated.

HAARIS: What about the beauty and the beautiful?

AALIF: Beauty is an illusion that eyes see and mind discerns—a serpent that looks charming but stings hard— a witch that tempts and damns. HAARIS: Some charms and illusions are necessary to live with. You are overthinking and overanalyzing. Overthinking begets complexity and complexity perturbs and destroys the beauty of life.

AALIF: *(laughs)* What is beauty and where is it? I can see no beauty nor can I feel its existence. You talk about beauty in life—the life that is a paralyzed force and creates the paralyzed who, with the desire of reproduction and for a little pleasure, keep on creating the crippled. Everyone suffers and creates more to suffer just for the instinct of pleasure. Many undergo the brutality of the powerful, many die craving for food, many perish in the pursuit of happiness, many bemoan being subjugated, many are ground in the grind of so called norms, taboos and ruthless customs of

society. The indispensable agonies— for one disobedience—- is not a fair deal.

HAARIS: But .... hmmm *(speechless)* AALIF: Would anyone like to have a child in such a terrible circumstance? What would be crueler? At least, I can't be that tyrant; I'm not going to have one.

HAARIS: But... what about the instinct to have sex and enjoy the pleasures of love making? Would you be able to brace your horse?

AALIF: I'll try to bridle my horse.

HAARIS: Yes, you'll have to. Your wife has a desire to reproduce and not to have sex only. AALIF: If I can control the desire deeply-rooted in humans that's to reproduce— I can do it as well. HAARIS: Desires and instincts are different, my dear. To have child is a desire but to have sex is an instinct.

Desires may be braced but not instincts.

AALIF: I will uproot the cause of the instinct.

HAARIS: Are you mad?

AALIF: Who denied? The wise crow sniffs the shit.

HAARIS: Yes. Exactly.

AALIF: Hmmm....

HAARIS: What?

AALIF: It's nothing! Is there something?
HAARIS: *(a bit infuriated)* Why are you doing all this? Why are you posing yourself to be a distinct and different fellow who gives a fuck to the society?

AALIF: Because society is a shit, one must give a fuck!

HAARIS: Then you are a shit on shit!

AALIF: *(mechanically laughs)* The chain of shit must be ceased!

HAARIS: Look dear! I like you for what you are and what you think but I suggest you to be a bit moderate, for an individual's colliding with the powerful norms of society is always disastrous; it can cost you your life. Why don't you understand this? Don't you see people dying either for their eccentric behaviors or for their indifference to societal set-up? They also die because they construct a point of view that seemingly collides with the religious values.

AALIF: Am I supposed to confirm to them? Is it profanity?

HAARIS: Hmmm... it is not but it could be labeled as one for it seems to be challenging the natural laws of free reproduction

AALIF: *(emotionally)* But it's all about me! It's my individuality! It's my decision! Am I not born with the privilege of being free?

HAARIS: You are not living in a jungle! AALIF: Huh! Tell me what difference will my not being productive make to the world where millions are desirous to reproduce?

HAARIS: I met your father. He is very much worried because he won't be able to have an heir and your point of view may spread in the community and may bring fatal consequences.

AALIF: What consequences?

HAARIS: It can spoil youth and, broadly speaking, it can cease. . . . everything AALIF: *(contemptuously)* You all think alike.

HAARIS: Whatever you say!

AALIF: Don't you think your given probability of ending everything is vague? How is it possible with single man's rebellion?

HAARIS: (loudly) People are suffering but many of them do not realize. If they happen to realize that they are suffering and your idea of not having a child strikes their mind, there could be a doom before doomsday.

AALIF: *(laughs hysterically)* You have gone too far. Do you think humans have power to do such a miracle? Alas! They don't have.

HAARIS: *(shrugs with an air of uncertainty)* It could be!
AALIF: If it is so, I must fire this idea.

HAARIS: Fuck off! *(he stares at him helplessly and leaves his room).*

(Aalif stares at the blank wall, he remains motionless for a while) AALIF:

Should I or Should I not?

The question hammers my mind

And inflicts my soul

I can't resist her innocently wild beauty

—The only thing that keeps my want-to-live

But my not having a child disturbs

The anatomy of my life; How can

she suppress her instinct?

Methinks she won't be able to.

What if she conditions for her desire?

Should I agree, or pretend to agree?

No , no , no, I would be a hypocrite!

But what of the erupting lava

That is burning my body

And agonizing my living?

Should I cut my genital,

The cause of contention?

No! My instinct does exist,

THE IMPOTENT

       At least I can quench it with that.
O what should I do!

Beseech her or masturbate?

Both are difficult acts;

One crushes my attitude

The other my taste

I think I should prefer instinct to attitude

ACT II SCENE I

The scene shifts to a spacious and simply but tastefully furnished room with only a bed and a cupboard. There are windows, one opening to a lush green lawn and a river-view, and the other to a congestedly housed populace. A cage with a pair of parrots is hanging near the window to the lawn. Nabigha is standing by the window looking outside. She is the embodiment of awesomeness, for her physique could make supermodels yearn to be like her and her looks are a strange amalgamation; sharp and seductive as well as patient and intelligent. While looking outside, she smiles but her smile seems to have weariness. Meanwhile, a parrot says something and she turns to it.

NABIGHA: *(looking at the pair of parrots with unshed tears)* Lucky you! Though caged, yet together!

PARROTS: *(talk)* Nabigha! Nabigha!

NABIGHA: Yes! Yes! Loneliness is like a hiss of a snake ambushed. It's horrific and horrible. The sound of the hidden menace spoils your peace of mind and is panicking enough to make you taste death before dying.

PARROTS: *(talk)* Death! Death! Death!

NABIGHA: Yes, it's death that could make a luminous star   fade,   a   flower wither, a luxuriant   unproductive, a land parched, a fertile infertile,   and a brave shiver.

(Parrots just squawk this time)

NABIGHA: *(gradually drenching into the emotional trance)* I'm , I'm bearing something worse than death— a state of being alone where I've no partner-like-partner, where my desires rise like a tsunami, knock violently for an outlet but I keep bracing them with the titanic walls of my patience. How long?

(she turns to the window to lawn, opens its panes and inhales fresh air.)

Why should I yield to this? He can't deprive me of the painfully beautiful experiences of life. I want it and I will get it.

(Meanwhile, there is a slight knock at the door and she starts)

NABIGHA: *(clearing her throat)* Who's there?

(Aalif comes in) NABIGHA: *(probingly)* Oh! You?

AALIF: Can't I?

NABIGHA: I didn't say that, but you usually don't.
AALIF: Hmm! I just wanted to see you.

NABIGHA: That's strange!

AALIF: *(whispers to himself)* How charming she is!

NABIGHA: What?

AALIF: Nothing

NABIGHA: Hmm! Okay

(Aalif goes near to her and grabs her waist)
NABIGHA: *(feeling ill at ease, she tries to release herself from his grip.)* Please Don't!

AALIF: I want to make love with you.

NABIGHA: *(hesitatingly)* No. That's not going to happen.

AALIF: Why not! You are my wife. Aren't you?

NABIGHA: Did you just realize?

AALIF: Realize? I know it!

NABIGHA: Lately, you have been treating me like a concubine. Your ferocious urge brings you to me. You can't brace it at all. How can you brace the most natural desire to be a father?

AALIF: Don't load things please.

NABIGHA: Oh! Saying things is like loading things? I'm a living being not dead and my desires must be revered.

AALIF: Don't you desire to make love?

NABIGHA: I do. But not in the way you want. You can have it fulfilled in many ways. Why do you need me then? Our relationship should keep its sanctity. Your coming here, having sex, and being off without respecting my desires makes it a kind of sacrilegious. Now that's not going to work.

AALIF: What do you want?

NABIGHA: *(at the verge of crying)* I'm desirous of being a mother.

AALIF: An instinct that brings pleasure is far better than the desire that may bring disaster. Why don't you choose sagaciously?

NABIGHA: Life can't be spent on what 'may bring disaster'. Your pleasure is my pleasure and your assumed 'disaster' is also my utmost pleasure. I am sagacious enough to double it if you want or I can sacrifice both.

AALIF: I'm dying for you.

NABIGHA: Not for me but for your passion.

AALIF: At least, once!

NABIGHA: Once keeps on and I'm not going to submit to this bloody 'once'.

AALIF: That's pathetic! Of the entire world, you are distinct for me. I'm neither self-conceited to treat you as my concubine, nor am I inhumane to use for the satisfaction of my carnival desires. I adore none but you for both your beauty and intelligence. No one else can incite me. Why do I come to you when I can go anywhere for quenching my thirst? Because you, only you, can satisfy me! Had I been assuming myself to be the powerful, I would have forced you to satisfy me. Have I ever forced a 'yes' out of you? Have I ever left you unsatisfied? Have you not been enjoying lovemaking? Don't pose to be a hypocrite. I thought you were the closest to me and you would understand the burdens and storms in my mind.

NABIGHA: I did enjoy your presence. I did enjoy every touch of yours that always left me mesmerized. I did relish your looking at me and smiling for me rather I've stored the treasure of your memories and the moments spent with you. Standing by the same window, I often become nostalgic and fondle with the beauty of the memories. I lull them as a mother does to a child. And yes, you were mentioning that you never forced me for love-making. True, but I also mentioned 'lately', you have not been making me feel your presence and touch. I think the losing of the desire for child makes you lose the passion of love making.

AALIF: I can strive to be the old being.

NABIGHA: How can you be that 'being' again when you have become an 'else'?

AALIF: Hmmmm! *(after a pause)* Some often assume their ego to be self-respect, and some other become so cynical that they mistreat themselves for the so-called prestige. I infer you are both

kinds.

NABIGHA: Don't be a judge!

AALIF: A judgment made at the spur is immoral. I know you for years.

NABIGHA: So do I!

AALIF: Judge me then! At least I'm not a hypocrite.

NABIGHA: Am I?

AALIF: Aren't you? Look at your face, it mirrors your physical demands. Aren't you going against the nature by suppressing what is natural and needs an outlet?

NABIGHA: *(with tears she turns to parrots and taps the bars of their cage)* You should go now.

AALIF: Ok, I'm going. I won't come to you ever again. But I promise I will, if I ever develop a desire for a child.

(He leaves, she sobs)

ACT II SCENE II

The scene shifts to a street, an overly messy and crowded area with tea stalls and pan shops; for the street is rough and unpaved with garbage alongside the drains. The buildings on the both sides of the streets are worn out (picturing post-apocalypse) projecting themselves as if bending to fall at any moment, the chairs of two tea stalls seem to be messed and mixed. Aalif is seen sitting alone at the table waiting for someone to take his orders and watching people laughing and gossiping. He, with his blank face and barren eyes, looks around and stares for quite a long time at children calling and attracting people for tea. After a long time of wait, a cute and innocent boy notices him and comes to him at his signal.

CHILD: *(inquiringly)* Yes sir!

AALIF: *(narrowing his eyes, he looks at child's face)* You are quite angelic!

CHILD: What sir?

AALIF: Nothing. What's your name?

CHILD: Bashar sir! Order please. My owner is watching and he will rebuke me for standing long and being late.

AALIF: You are already much late, my boy!

[pause]

Bring me a cup of strong tea with no sugar.

CHILD: *(he moves back)* Ok sir.

AALIF: *(talks to himself)* This is pathetic. I grieve for the innocence being exploited in such a chaos. They ask me to bring a child in this muddled world. Why the hell would I, when millions like him are already bemoaning and bewailing in this ruthless world? Look! How the innocent kids are suppressed for a piece of bread. Getting the piece of bread for them and their family is the sole purpose of their life. Is life so trivial? Can life be so frivolous to be spent for bread? I don't understand how people dare bring so many children in the world when they themselves have nothing to live on. That's ignorance! Utter ignorance! But I'm not ignorant.

(The boy brings him a cup of tea) CHILD: Here is your tea, sir.

AALIF: *(starts)* Oh! Tea.

(Aalif looks at him again and his eyes shift downward from his face to his rags, then to his little feet filled with dirt. Tears, while looking at him, gradually grow and flow from his eyes. He tries to hide his tears by

looking downwards. Having wiped them with the palms of his hands, he looks up).

Thank you!

(A group of four young boys sit at the table next to him. They all use their cell phones for quite a time. One of them breaks the silence)

BOY I: You could use your phones at home. What the hell are we doing here?

BOY II: I was checking out some videos on Tiktok.

BOY III: I thought to check my WhatsApp status.

BOY II: Whatever! Now throw them aside.

BOY IV: A girlfriend could contact.

(All laugh) BOY I: She can wait for a while

BOY IV: Girls don't wait nowadays.

BOY II: *(winks)* But your girlfriend is very hot buddy!

BOY IV: *(laughs)* Yes, she is!

BOY III: *(pretending to be sad)* My girlfriend was hot too and left me for a hot boy. I am girlfriendless these days. Kindly help me out in getting one.

BOY II: We don't run a market.

BOY III: *(giving him a crooked smile)* You are quite rich but you don't share even the slightest of your relations with female. You are such a mean.

> *(All laugh)*

BOY II: I've saved them for my rainy days. BOY III: You are my friend. Won't you help me in my rainy days?

BOY I: Can you ever talk about something other than girls?

BOY II: Don't preach morality. Had you one, you would have bragged the most. Only lack of something incites morality in you.

BOY I: Had I ever tried, I would have many. BOY II: You have tried a lot but you have none. You are still trying, I know. Keep trying unless you get   one.

BOY I: You are mean-spirited

BOY III: This is life, my dear. Enjoy it to its fullest. It's not man who is the crown of creation but woman, and around her revolves the world.

> *(While taking sips of his tea, Aalif overhears them and passes an unconvinced smile)*

> *[pause]*

(He calls the little boy, Bashar) BASHAR: Yes sir.

AALIF: *(gives him a hundred rupee note)* Keep the change.

BASHAR: *(humbly)* Thank you, sir!
(He leaves the table and walks numbly to the pan shop a few yards away from the tea stalls. It's 'Madni Pan Shop' where an old yet stout fellow with white beard, head covered with a Sindhi cap, is standing behind the counter. His fingers and lips are red for he remains busy in preparing and chewing pans)

AALIF: Chacha, how are you doing?

CHACHA: Everything is good by the grace of Allah.

AALIF: Kindly, prepare and pack my pan.

(Chacha says something with his mouth full of pan).

AALIF: Sorry?

CHACHA: *(spits into 'pandan')* Where have you been? Long time, no see.

AALIF: *(seriously)* Sometimes, life neither moves nor lets us move.

CHACHA: *(busy in making pan)* Wait and have faith in

Allah.

AALIF: (his eyes shift to the group of boys who are still laughing and smiling). How can one be that happy in this life?

CHACHA: What happened, son?

AALIF: (pointing to them) Look at the boys. They have been laughing purposelessly for quite a time. I don't understand what is there to laugh in life. They are ignorant. They are not aware of the bitterness of life.

CHACHA: This is the blessing of ignorance. Don't overthink, son! Life is simple. Be simple and be happy. You can just look at the world, you can't change or stop it.

AALIF: Would that I could be happy! CHACHA: I have heard some discussions about you rebellious thinking of not having child in the mosque and among the elderly people of our community. I'm afraid there could be a severe reaction. Son! I suggest you to be conscious of this and change your attitude a bit. We cannot rebel against Allah, the Almighty. AALIF: Let them say whatever! I care the damn! I'm not rebelling against anyone.

(He pays, takes his pans and leaves).

ACT II SCENE III

The scene is in the TV lounge in Aalif's house where his father is smoking 'Huqqa' and his mother is knitting and watching TV. Aalif's father is muscular person with grave and mature looks. The wrinkles on his face are hardly visible. He takes a long puff and exhales with a sigh.

FATHER: I'm much worried about Aalif.

MOTHER: Has he said something wrong again?

FATHER: He is the only son and its disappointing that he is not willing to give us our grandson to extend our family line.

MOTHER: Yes, it is disappointing enough to bring about distress but I will surely try to convince him otherwise.

FATHER: He was stubborn but now he has become quite indifferent as well.

MOTHER: I know but he is my son. I know how to trigger his emotions and convince him.

(Aalif enters from the main gate and passes from courtyard without looking at them and bothering their presence)

FATHER: Aalif! Come here.
AALIF: Yes, Father.

(He sits) FATHER: *(gently)* Where have you been?

AALIF: Outside.

FATHER: Listen my son! I am quite perturbed because of your indifferent attitude. You have assumed and made up the world that fits you only and you are not willing to come out of it. MOTHER: Son! Look at us, look at our ages. We also have dreams. Don't bash our dreams of becoming grandparents. I beseech you, fulfill this desire so that we could die in peace.

AALIF: I salute your courage to bring me to this world but I have my reservations.

FATHER: I beg you to change your mind. AALIF: Don't push me into it. I'm already bothered about

'to be'.

FATHER: Things are not the way you perceive them. The world seems ugly to you for you seem to see only ugliness in it and you have magnified the ugliness to live in it. The world is battered, I know. It has ugliness, I also know but there is plenty to relish; some bits of happiness that are enough to live with, like becoming a parent. My happiness knew no bounds when you were born. Then your innocent smile, your calling me papa, your playing with me and, later, your success in education multiplied it. You can never realize it unless you become a parent. I have lived through you, you will live through your child.

(Silence for a while) MOTHER: Without becoming a parent you are depriving yourself of the feel that some may enjoy as a zenith of love. Our life was bad if we hadn't you. If you don't have a child, yours will be, too.

AALIF: Bringing me in the world was your happiness you've been enjoying I've been suffering. Bringing my child in this world may be my happiness or yours but not his. I can foresee what you didn't. You can't reach the profoundness of my thought, I am alone on this agonizing journey.

FATHER: But.....

(A knock at the door is heard, Aalif gets up to answer it).

Wait, let me get this.

(He goes, opens the door and sees some elderly man of the community. They say something to Aalif's father and he comes back with a sad face) MOTHER: *(inquiringly)* Is everything ok?

FATHER: *(shaking his head)* Our fears were right!

(Mother gets lifeless with a shock) AALIF: What fear?

FATHER: The people of community are calling both of us for a meeting.

AALIF: Meeting about what?

FATHER: I'm afraid, it's about your odd behavior.

AALIF: Odd? *(tries to understand)* Oh! No problem! I'll see them.

(He gets up and leaves)

(Father shouts at his back)

This is the problem, but you don't realize.

ACT III SCENE I

The scene is set in an open space at Chaudry Rahimdad's Haveli— an exhibition of tradition-- where the lawn is full of trees, plants and flower-beds. In the center, there is a big grassy area where cots of huge size with two big cushions on each are set in a rectangle shape. The big gate of Haveli is open and two bullterrier dogs are chained nearby, they bark at everyone coming in. Chaudry Rahimdad, a tall middle-aged man with dark black dyed mustaches, bulging eyes and a large round belly is wearing white 'Shalwar Kameez' a turban and a 'Khussa'. He is sitting on a cot facing the gate with Professor Shamsi and Molvi Nazeer in the right row and Aalif, his father and Haaris with his son, Aadam, on the left. The cot in front of Chaudry Rahimdad is empty. Some tenants, servants and people of common ranks (like Cobblers, Panwalas, Tenants, Barbers) are standing behind the cots. Meanwhile, they all stand in respect when a young man with some of his devotees arrives. Chaudry Sahib receives him, kisses his hand, leaves his place for him and goes to the right row to Molvi Sahib. While the man motions all to sit, his lips are moving and his hands rolling beads of rosary. He looks very healthy with a glowing red face that wears a beard of formal cut. His devotees stand behind him with their heads down.

(After a brief silence)

CHAUDRY SAHIB: *(to the young man)* Am I permitted to start Shah Ji?

(Shah Ji nods his head).

CHAUDRY SAHIB: I begin in the name of Allah, the most compassionate, the most merciful. You all know what we are here for. In fact, there are complaints against Aalif for his being secular and liberal. But I am a kind of person who avoids hearsays. Therefore, I called for Aalif for his point of view and the rest for theirs and requested Shah Ji to guide us spiritually in this matter. *(to*

Molvi Sahib) What is the complaint Molvi Sahib? MOLVI SAHIB: Chaudry Ji, the assault of western civilization and culture with its philosophies of liberalism and secularism is devastating our religious, cultural and moral values. With his western knowledge and no Islamic knowledge, Aalif has become one of their representatives. His ideas are non-religious and they are spoiling the young of our community. CHAUDRY SAHIB: What ideas? Can you please be specific?

MOLVI SAHIB: He is contradicting our religious values for he believes and preaches the idea of having no child. Isn't he going against nature?

(Shah Ji seems shocked) CHAUDRY SAHIB: Is it right, Aalif?

AALIF: Yes, to an extent.

CHAUDRY SAHIB: Don't play riddles!

THE IMPOTENT

AALIF: This is my personal belief; it is not harmful for society because I don't preach it. I don't talk to people about it but if I do, I tell them about my belief and do not force them to follow it. MOLVI SAHIB: Humans are fascinated by the opposite and even Satan helps if it diverts them to a sin. Whatever you are saying is categorically a sin. It will catch fire rather it is catching fire. Your hellish idea needs no preaching, its being conveyed to people is preaching in itself. European 'marriages' are already in.

AALIF: Molvi Ji! You are deliberately making it a sin. Is it a sin to deliver someone from fever and fret of the world? How fragile are your norms and beliefs!

MOLVI SAHIB: *(aggressively)* Who has given you the authority? Are you messiah or what?

PROFESSOR: You are misconstruing. Try to understand what he is saying. You are taking on one strand while he is another. It will complicate things.

AALIF: *(avoids Molvi Ji and talks to Professor).* What do I have to be authoritative of? I am the protector of my child like every other father. Having brought them into the world, they try to protect them but, as it seems to me, they get failed mostly and they   along with their children suffer incessantly. I've decided not to repeat the mistake of others.

FATHER: Do you think yourself a mistake of mine?

AALIF: Yes! A big mistake!

MOLVI SAHIB: *(getting beside himself)* Shah Ji, Chaudry Sahib! Look at his insolence. He is calling the creation of Allah a mistake. He is finding faults with the best of the best. Western ideas have turned his head. Bridle him or he will be a contagious infection to the society and we know how to bridle such sacrilegious man.

> *(Shah Ji nods and people standing there start whispering aloud and Chaudry Sahib tries to silence them)*

HAARIS: (a bit loud) Molvi Ji, you're going to the extremes. What are we here for? We are here to discuss and find a solution. You are giving your judgmental decision and not arguing to convince. *(Aadam looks at his father when he speaks and turns to Molvi Sahib when he does)*

MOLVI SAHIB: *(recites a verse)* "They are deaf, dumb and blind. So they will not return (to the right path)." He is beyond persuasion. Such people should be treated in a way...... you better know. Such rioters are not needed in the peaceful realms of Allah.

(All people there say: Yes, indeed! Yes, indeed!)
HAARIS: You don't know hearts only Allah (the best guide) does. Aalif is not a rioter but a 'lost sheep'. He is...

(Professor intervenes)

PROFESSOR: We are not here to win the argument but to solve the problem. And Molvi Sahib, I'm not sure whether his ideas create riot or not but your aggression will, certainly.

MOLVI SAHIB: But the fact of the matter....

(Chaudry Sahib motions him to stay clam!)
CHAUDRY SAHIB: Society is the store house of all the cherished values. In one way or the other, we have to defend these values.

(to Shah Ji) You are the most sagacious and spiritually powerful amongst us. Please, find us a way and guide us to it.

(After a minute of silence)

SHAH JI: He has no *Murshad* and a person without *Murshad* is like a boat without sailor. *(to Aalif, in   a resonant voice)* Go find a *Murshad* and pledge allegiance to him.

AALIF: *(whispers to himself)* I know these so called *Murshads* and their deeds.

SHAH JI: *(grins)* What?

AALIF: I'm the sailor of my own boat and I know my directions too.

DEVOTEE: Shut your mouth, you insolent! CHAUDRY SAHIB: *(to Aalif)* Behave yourself and show some respect.

MOLVI SAHIB: *(loudly)* I have already defined him. PROFESSOR: *(to Aalif)* I know you are compassionate for the world and for your unborn child but the world is not what you think of it, it is what it is.

 Being philosophic is good but being too philosophic or too conscious is dangerous. As I can see your too much inclination to philosophy, let me tell you, dear brother, the philosophies are on or about human beings—human beings create them but your too much inclination make you a product of philosophy.

AALIF: You are mistaken, Professor! I am not the product of any philosophy rather I have created one and

THE IMPOTENT

I am courageous enough to live with it. And if one is too conscious, one can't help being so.

PROFESSOR: All right, you are a great man and you have created a philosophy. What's the use of the philosophy that complicates your life and the lives of the people dear to you? Bumping into a wall hurts you and you only.

AALIF: Life is complicated with or without a philosophy. When you hurt yourself against your will, why not bump into walls and hurt with a will? PROFESSOR: There is no use of chewing something if you know you cannot digest it.

AALIF: *(jokingly)* I have a good digestive system.

PROFESSOR: To satisfy your will, you are going against the will of God and making the people around you unhappy. My dear! Many philosophers and scholars question the purpose of existence and meaningfulness of life. I believe, reproducing, as every living organism does, gives purpose and meaning to your life. Unconsciously, owing to your rebellion against a simple natural law, you are losing the purpose of your existence. AALIF: I am not concerned about every living organism but myself I know the hellish life I am living. PROFESSOR: *(irritatingly)* How cowardly and sniveling you are as you are letting you down, going deep down in a hopeless abyss. Better than you are the penguins who, in spite of deadening cold, the menace of being hunted or dying of hunger, save their eggs to have their chicks. Don't they sacrifice? Don't they have fears?

MOLVI SAHHIB: Even Allah forbids being fearful regarding your children. "And   kill   not   your children for fear of poverty— we provide for   them and for you."

(Aalif stands up)

AALIF: *(with an air of sadness)* Why don't you leave me with what I have? Why are you so interested in my producing a child? *(to Molvi Sahib)* Do you mean that I am a killer? We kill what is alive and I don't want him to be alive for he would be killed (tears roll down from his eyes) ---he would either be suffocated by your so-called created norms or by an enemy.

[pause]

(to Professor) I'm not coward, Sir, I'm just ultracautious. Are you not aware of the monstrous world where the powerful are crushing the innocent or the hypocritical societies, where these Hypocrites are ruling *(motions to Shah Ji, Molvi*

Sahib, and Chaudry Sahib) and crushing the sundry? Far isn't the time when you, me will become irrelevant, undesired, unwanted.

[pause]

You never say no to the offering of your devotees and you are thriving along with your businesses but the majority of your devotees are thinning down. O Pharos of the earth! Have you ever sent meals to their houses? If you are chosen, what are they? Doubtless! You won't challenge the system you are beneficiary of.

(Few of the onlookers shout at him) MAN 1: Zip your mouth or we'll wring your tongue out   of it.

MAN 2: He is our Murshad-e-Kamil.

MAN 3: *(aggressively)* I will rip you pieces, you deviator.
(Dogs bark)

FATHER: *(observing people's reaction)* Sit down, Aalif.
AALIF: *(to Chaudry Sb)* And you......

FATHER: *(drags his arm)* I say, sit down! Why are you dragging me into dirt?

(Aadam puts fingers in his ears and hides his face into his father's chest. Aalif looks at him and stares at him for a moment)

AALIF: *(releasing his arms from his father's grip)* Let me speak. *(to Chaudry Sahib again)* Look at the sunken faces of your tenants and servants *(points to some of them)*. Have you never thought of their children's future? Instead of blood, sweat runs into their veins, even then, they won't be able to brighten the dark life of their offspring. Are you concerned about me, my father or the people gathered around? Not at all, it is just a show off. In fact, dear to you is your political career, love you more not them but their votes.

(All eyes turn to Chaudry Sahib who himself is shocked)?

The world may have been a better place if the leeches like you all have not come into existence MOLVI SAHIB: ...ولا حول You are defiant and disrespectful to your elders and religio-societal values. Allah's fury will fall on you.

AALIF: *(in a low tone)* Ain't you afraid of Allah's fury *(raising his voice)* You exploit the innocent children of your madrassa and involve in bloody 'rites'. I'm not hypocrite; I'll call a spade a spade. Through your misinterpretation, you misguide your disciples. The like of you have played your full role in making this society a hell. If you seek to blow me up, blow me up with your arguments. I'm done with the recurrent threat of your inferno.

(Turns his face from Molvi Sahib to all and raises his voice to a slight shout)
Do I hurt you? What harm is it to you if I do not produce a child? Will my child be a chosen one? I don't understand why you are keeping an eye on me? Is this how a society works—crushing an individual and snatching his freedom? *(He almost cries).* I feel suffocated among you. What's the necessity of my bringing child into the world? I feel like, at times, asking my father why he brought me into this world. It wasn't a necessity. Even your being here is not a necessity. *(He cries like a child, wiping his tears, he leaves through the main gate).*

(Silence prevails for a while then the dogs bark)
FATHER: *(touching Shah Ji's knees)* I beg forgiveness for him. I beg forgiveness. I'm low, you're high. SHAH

JI: Riaz, don't beg for him, he is cancerous! His howls must be responded.

FATHER: Mercy, Shah Ji, mercy! He's my only son.

>*(Chaudry taps his hand and motions him to leave)*

>*(Aalif's father along with Haaris and his child, leaves)*

ACT III SCENE II

The scene is in Aalif's room where he is sitting on the floor sobbing and smoking. He rests his head on the couch nearby and sleeps. After a while he springs up. AALIF:

Closing my eyes for a while, I dreamt

Helpless and half-dead did I lie

On the scorching sand

That was melting my skin

From nowhere did there come

Some vultures utterly ugly

They pounced upon me

With their beaks snatching my flesh.

They ate to their choice;

One filched my eyes,

The other fused my thinking

They altogether tore my heart

And celebrated with it

As if it were the totem of their efforts.

Though I'm awake, I'm restless

For I have understood the message of it.

(Footsteps are heard outside)

AALIF: *(hysterically)* I think they are coming for me. (AALIF's father, Haaris and his child enter) FATHER: What have you done?

(*He remains silent and gazes at Haaris'son*) HAARIS: Uncle, what's done is done. We should be ready for their reaction and should do something to save him. *(to Aalif)* I think you should come with me to my house for a few days.

AALIF: *(turns a deaf ear to him and observes the child's face)* Why did you take Aadam to such a hell? HAARIS: Oh! He is much attached. He persists being with me everywhere.

AALIF: How innocent he is!

HAARIS: *(worriedly)* Aalif, let's go! They could be here any moment.

FATHER: *(showing concern)* Yes, my son, go with him. AALIF: I'm not going anywhere.

HAARIS: Try to...... *(they hear doorbell ringing noisily)* .... *(lowering his voice)* understand.

(*Aalif's father goes out to answer the bell and Haaris keeps a watch standing in the door from where he could see the main gate. He sees a man, along with many, pushing Aalif's father away and getting into the courtyard).*

MAN 1: *(shouts)* Come out, come out, you insolent coward. How dare you use derogatory language against our values and our elders! *(Haaris stops Aalif in the doorway but he tries to make his way out).*

MAN 2: Drag the mouse out of his molehill.

(Aalif comes out with Haaris and his child behind)

AALIF: What ails you all?

MAN 1: *(he commands all)* Grab the dog!

(One of the men aggressively moves forward, grabs his arm, drags him to the other man and gives him the first slap. The others pounce upon him and start hitting without a concession. He falls to the ground, but they mercilessly kick and punch him and he quails his body. They have surrounded him in such a way that the screams of his father and his friend and the wailing of his mother and wife cannot save him. Haaris and Aalif's father, in their struggle to pull the people away, receive many blows. Their struggle goes in vain. His clothes turned rags, his body is badly wounded and his face though besmeared in blood is still neutral. They beat him until he stirs no more. They leave him half dead.)

MAN 1: *(threatens)* Beware of babbling against Shah Ji or you will have more in future.

> *(People go out of the house)*

> *(Aalif's father and mother, Haaris, Nabigha rush to him, lift him and put him onto the cot nearby)*

MOTHER: *(shouts)* Bring water, bring water for him. *(Nabigha runs and fetches water. They all make him drink water)*

HAARIS: That's what I was afraid of.

MOTHER: *(sobs)* Look, what they have done to him.

> *(Nabigha speaks nothing but tears roll down her eyes. Aalif is startled and looks around. Meanwhile, Haaris' son, Aadam moves to him)* AADAM: *(touches Aalif's forehead)* Uncle, you are bleeding. *(to Haaris)* Papa! Take him to the doctor uncle.

HAARIS: Yes, son, we will.

AADAM: Uncle, you'll be fine, don't worry. *(Aalif grabs his tiny hand, struggles to get up and takes him into his arms for quite a while)* AALIF: Sweet is your touch!

ACT III SCENE III

After 15 days, the scene is set in Nabigha's room where she is standing near the window to the lawn. The weather outside is cool. She's leaning against the window and enjoying the breeze—brushing her cheeks and fluttering her hair.

>*(Aalif comes in and she turns her head to him)*

AALIF: *(feels the cool breeze)* Enjoying weather?

NABIGHA: It's quite pleasing today.

AALIF: *(going to the window)* It seems to be. NABIGHA: *(with an air of curiosity)* What brought you here?

AALIF: I wanted to see you.

>*(She smiles)*

>You look beautiful when you smile. With the spreading of your lips, your cheeks get dimpled and your eyes with glitter respond equally.

NABIGHA: *(with a smile)* Don't exaggerate!

AALIF: You have charms, Nabigha.

NABIGHA: *(blushes)* You have eyes, Aalif. I'm glad you can see me again.

AALIF: *(hesitatingly)* I want a child.

NABIGHA: *(shocked)* What! Say it again, for it pleases my ears and relieves my soul.

AALIF: I want a child with you.
NABIGHA: I'm happy that you have finally realized it.

AALIF: Yes!

NABIGHA: How did it happen?

AALIF: "Had enough of heartbreak and pain

Had a little sweet spot for the rain."

Our impulses determine our do's and don'ts and impulses could be triggered by anything; may be a portrait, or an innocent face, or *(jokingly)* enchanting deep, black eyes like yours.

NABIGHA: *(with a dim smile)* Interesting!

AALIF: *(emotionally)* You know, Nabigha, I spent last fifteen days on bed in a severe pain, not because of physical wounds but because I have had an epic struggle with me— between my impulses and rationality. My impulses won and I thought to have my Aadam.

NABIGHA: *(amazed)* Aadam?

AALIF: I mean a child.

NABIGHA: The beating worked!

(They both laugh)

AALIF: *(gets serious)* The corporal beatings can't beat me, do you think the beating changed me?

NABIGHA: *(jokingly)* I think it did this time.

AALIF: *(he smiles vaguely)* No way.
NABIGHA: I was joking, it's been long I didn't. *(grabs his hand)* I know you very well.

AALIF: Thank you.

NABIGHA: Anyways, it's a great metamorphosis.

AALIF: *(gets closer and whispers)* A kind of.

NABIGHA: After such a storm!

AALIF: A calm after a storm!

> *(He gently dashes his head against hers and they both smile)*

ACT III SCENE IV

The scene opens in a doctor's clinic. Aalif and Nabigha as the first patients are waiting for the doctor and talking to each other in a low voice. Various pictures of pregnant mothers and newborn babies are pasted on the walls. Aalif takes a panoramic view of the room and Nabigha seems to be observing the movement of his eyes. Aalif's face looks calm and serious but Nabigha's curious. AALIF: *(looking at one of the pictures on the wall)* That's cute! Nabigha, our baby would be even cuter.

NABIGHA: Yes, if he or she takes after me.

(They laugh)

But I want his or her eyes like yours. AALIF: Nabigha, I took a daring step to be a father. I'm very anxious as well as afraid. NABIGHA: Come on, be optimistic, it will be fine. You   just……

(The door opens, the doctor comes in and exchanges greetings)

DOCTOR: What's the matter?

NABIGHA: I did not have my menstrual cycle this month and we thought to consult.

DOCTOR: What's your date?

NABIGHA: I'm five days late.

DOCTOR: It could be a good piece of news or just hormonal disturbance. Can you please go and   check?

(She hands her a strip)

(She goes to the washroom while Aalif seems a bit restless and his left leg is shivering. Nabigha comes out of the washroom and returns the strip to the doctor)

DOCTOR: *(observes)* It's negative. *(after a pause)* Did you have intercourse daily?

NABIGHA: *(shyly)* Yes.

AALIF: (confidently) With the exception of few days, we remained continuous.

DOCTOR: *(giggles)* I'm writing some further tests for both of you. *(she writes TSH, FSH, PRL for Nabigha and Sperm Count Test for Aalif).* Kindly go to the lab and come back to me with the reports.

(Both of them come back after getting their reports and show them the doctor. She studies Nabigha's report first)

DOCTOR: It's quite normal but only TSH is a little high.

You will be all right with some medicines
(She picks up Aalif's reports and starts studying them. After a while, she puts it down) NABIGHA: Is everything all right?

DOCTOR: *(to Aalif)* I'm really sorry, you cannot be a father. You are absolutely infertile.

(Aalif remains expressionless) NABIGHA: This is not possible.

(After a pause)

There may be a remedy, Doctor. Something you could do.

(She begs)

DOCTOR: There is nothing I can do. Pray to God. Miracles happen.

(Aalif gazes at the doctor for some moments, smiles, holds the sobbing Nabigha's hand, and leaves the room)

THE END

www.ingramcontent.com/pod-product-compliance
Lightning Source LLC
Chambersburg PA
CBHW020749160726
47993CB00006B/2689